A Soldi

Mary Lou Lang and William Lang III

A Soldier's Journey

William M. Lang III and Mary Lou Lang

DEDICATION

To James, Rosanne, Brendan and Mathew Lang who left us too soon

ACKNOWLEDGEMENTS

We would like to thank many who made this book possible. To Paula, whose endless devotion and support could never be repaid, and to my children, Sean, Meghan and Shanna, for their loyalty. To Ryan and Colin for their encouragement and support—life would be meaningless without you. To our family and friends who supported this book and who continue to grace our lives, we thank you. Special thanks also to Anthony Falconeri for his time editing this book.

CONTENTS

1 COMES A HERO

He came wailing into the world on a cold November day in 1924, five years before the Great Depression and the stock market crash. He weighed 7 pounds when he was born at 2:30 a.m. on the 30th, and while his birth was without complication, the future 91 years of William Lang Jr.'s life would lack simplicity and be considered amazing by the estimation of many.

When his mother pulled her newborn child into her arms for the first time to bond, he stopped wailing. Soon thereafter, the midwife took her pay and left the family of four.

William, also called Billy, was the second son of William and Mary Agnes. His brother Joseph, born 18 months earlier, rounded out the group. They were good Catholics and a new life meant another start for a brighter future.

Playing the baby's weight, birthdate or time born with a bookie and the three-digit number, derived from the newspaper, could pay five hundred to one. Mary and William Sr. would repeat the process a total of ten times, when their youngest child Michael was born in 1940.

They unfortunately never hit the number with the bookie.

The stock market crash didn't affect this poor family until 1930 when their father and breadwinner lost his job. Most people could not find work, and it seemed everyone was scratching, hustling and clawing just to survive. But somehow the kids never went hungry. The Lang family always found a way to put food on the table even though many times the parents went without dinner.

Billy and his siblings' formative years were spent living in severe hardship. Although the streets held pitfalls and danger, they also provided for redemption from hunger. There were also friends who always had your back, and you in turn had theirs.

The neighborhood kids were tough, not just in body but also in mind. In 1936 and subsequent years, they found themselves hustling for food and working hard. Most days the children would check in with Henri in the deli and Joe the butcher for the ends of the baloney. All the processed meat that was sliced to make sandwiches and platters ended when the meat in the package could no longer be sliced. So baloney, liverwurst, ham, salami and processed cheese had two ends that normally would be trashed. The neighborhood kids made sure the ends went into bellies and not into the garbage pails.

The bakery was also another gold mine where the children could find riches beyond what they expected. The bakery discarded a product if it stayed on the shelf for more than two days. The bread and cake that did not sell on the first day were marked down and sold at a discount on the second day. After that, if the product didn't sell it was marked to be discarded. The children in the neighborhood, once again, were there to be sure that the products were consumed.

Nothing went to waste. "Hell," the kids thought, "if bread or cake had some green growth on it, it was still good after you cut the mold from it and toasted it."

Michie's, the neighborhood fruit stand, was another place the kids had their sights set on when they were hungry. But Michie proved he was smart to their antics, and he would stand guard over his fruits and vegetables displayed outside of the store.

Still the neighborhood kids were able to outsmart the fruit stand owner. The kids would work out a scheme to make Michie look one way while those on the backside relieved him of some fruits and vegetables.

The best from the stand were the potatoes. When wrapped in foil and placed into a fire down in the 17th Street lots, they came out as Mickeys and were absolutely the best tasting potato outside of Nathan's French fries in Coney Island.

Having great tasting Mickeys created another issue: The bigger neighborhood boys would show up when the Mickeys were about to come out of the fire. They would push the little boys away and help themselves to the feast. It was survival for everyone and the bullies would have the edge.

The little boys would learn from being bullied. Their answer was to take a potato skin, wrap it around dog shit, and place it strategically in the fire where only the boys who did the work knew not to touch it.

Like clockwork, one of the meanest guys who was freest with his hands on anyone smaller got the prize. While he unwrapped the foil, the little guys kept him distracted so he would not inspect the purloined potato. When the bully took a healthy bite and began to chew, the little guys booked and laughed as the realization dawned on the bully that it was not a potato he was chewing.

These difficult years certainly played a role in Billy's military life, giving him the courage, stamina, fortitude and characteristics he needed to survive the deadliest battle of World War II, his subsequent capture by the Nazis, and his eight months of survival as a prisoner of war in one of the worst prison camps in Germany.

2 GROWING UP ON THE HILL

Park Slope, Brooklyn, an area known as "The Hill", is the highest point in Kings County. The neighborhood, nestled between Prospect Park and Greenwood Cemetery, had dwellings consisting of four-story apartment buildings, brownstones, and single-family attached houses.

Enclaves of Irish, Polish and Italian immigrants were mixed throughout the area. The public schools of the neighborhood were PS 10, PS 154, and Manual Training High School. Holy Name Catholic Church and school ministered to the bulk of first- and second-generation Catholic immigrants. The school taught to its capacity of 1,600 girls and boys separated from grades one through eight.

The Sisters of St. Joseph taught the lower grades of the boys' and girls' classes. The smarter and more affluent children went on to Catholic high schools. Xaverian Brothers taught the boys in grades six, seven and eight. Neither order believed that corporal punishment of students was wrong. In fact, spare the rod and spoil the child was their mandate and no child would be spoiled in Holy

Name. If you came home after you received corporal punishment in school another beating was waiting for you there.

All of Billy Sr. and Mary Agnes' children began at Holy Name, although a few did not finish as they were asked to withdraw for various reasons. The main reason many were asked to leave was for nonpayment of tuition.

All the children of Holy Name would attend the nine o'clock mass on Sunday mornings. Because the parish was one of the largest in New York, the pastor was a bishop. In the days before microphones and speakers, the bishop came with a prerequisite—a loud and booming voice.

Every Sunday just before church dismissal the names of those with delinquent tuition would be shouted out by the bishop in alphabetical order. When he got to the L's you would hear Lang, six to eight times in succession. "Lang, Lang, Lang…", boomed the bishop, as anyone with that surname tried to shrink into the pews.

The neighborhood children were the second generation of numerous nationalities and each group fought for supremacy in the streets. Fighting for the honor of one's family was expected. A misdirected slur or a purposely directed insult to a family member most likely ended in broken bones and bloody noses. This was a time before political correctness, and the terms "Donkey," "Wop," "Pollock," "Chink," "Jews," "Spicks," and "Niggers" were also openly spoken in the streets.

Most of the single combat fights were held at a particular time and place. Once word got out, curious onlookers would fill the streets in anticipation. You made your bones here. You took your beatings and sometimes beat others. But if you were to be respected, you knew you had to show up to the fight and bring your all. You went as hard and as long as you could to make sure the other person would think twice about coming at you again.

Billy's street name was Tippy, and he was wiry tough and fast—another skill that would serve him well in his future with the U.S. Army. He could hit you three times before you even threw a punch. His fists were like rocks and his targets were your eyes and throat. His mantra was blind 'em, take away their wind, move in and out, be brave enough to go inside and don't be grabbed.

If the bigger street kids got their hands on you, they could make you suffer. So Billy knew he wouldn't let that happen. He learned, like others in the neighborhood that his reputation would go a long way to avoid confrontation.

By the time he was 14, Billy had gained a reputation in the streets as someone not to be messed with. He and his brother Joe defended their younger siblings until they became of age to fight their own battles. Others in the neighborhood knew it was a losing proposition to mess with the Lang boys because if you fought one you had to fight them all.

Aside from learning how to fill his belly and fight to survive in the streets of Park Slope, Billy and the other kids on the Hill amused themselves by playing the normal street games that were popular in their time. Johnny on the Pony, Coco Levio and Cowboys and Indians were the typical choice.

Prospect Park in the Spring signaled the end of winter by the greening of the grass fields and the baseball outfield grew in thick. In early May, the fields would be ready to play on. Baseball tryouts drew over 250 kids to fill a roster of twenty-five. The desire to play baseball was fueled by the fanatic love of the Brooklyn Dodgers in Ebbets Field, which was only a short trolley car ride away.

Prospect Park in the winter was also the neighborhood kids' playground and in the snow some would sleigh ride on Suicide Hill. Toward the bottom of Suicide Hill was a hump, and if you hit it at just the right angle, the rider would go airborne with their sleigh. If the hump was missed, the sleigh would be separated from the rider and each would go in different directions. If you were riding double or three to a sled, bodies flew in every direction. A cast on an arm, wrist or a leg were worn like a badge of honor. It was a testament to the courage that Suicide Hill took another victim who was brave enough to take her on.

In the summer, stickball and stoop ball were the chosen games. Some stickball games were played in the street and the sewers served as the bases. A really good hitter was said to be a "four sewers guy."

On really hot days, a wrench was used to open the fire hydrant, also called the Johnny Pump. The neighbor-hood kids used a can, cut open at both ends, to direct the water at cars that drove by and even at people who walked within target distance. Though the children thought it was funny, those who were hit with a full force of water thought that the kids were punks.

The police were typically called to shut off the open hydrant. If the pump was left open for more than an hour, top floor apartments would have no water because of the reduced pressure.

Another area where Billy and the other neighborhood kids would play was Greenwood Cemetery, renowned for its unique architecture and notable people buried there. It was surrounded by eight-foot iron fences with sharp-spiked tops designed to keep out trespassers and preserve the sanctity of the cemetery.

To the neighborhood kids, it was the ultimate playground.

When the kids (usually about a group 25 or more) found an opening in the fence that they could squeeze through, they played Hide and Seek among the grave stones and mausoleums.

The avoidance of being captured by the other team was a challenge, but being caught by the cemetery custodians was even worse. They would surround the children and five grown men would capture one or two of the slowest kids and beat the shit out of them. They would turn them over to the police who wrote them up and gave them a "juvenile delinquent" or "JD" card.

Getting a juvenile delinquent card was a serious infraction. Multiple violations could put a boy away for a year in the juvenile detention facility. Any kid going to what the neighborhood boys called Juvie would spend at least a year away from their family. Not a single child they knew who went to Juvie was the same going in as he was when he came out.

3 THE TEENAGE YEARS

By the time Billy was 14 he had six siblings and a rough life was the only life that the Lang children knew. One day that was celebrated with a feast was Saint Patrick's Day, and in 1938 the typical dinner and parties in the neighborhood were planned.

But on that particular Saint Patrick's Day, the Lang family experienced tragedy beyond comprehension. Billy's young three-year-old brother, Walter, reached up on the stove and pulled a pot of corned beef and cabbage down upon himself.

He died three days later.

It was a loss that Billy's family never really recovered from although they took solace knowing he was with God. Billy's mother taught the children to pray the rosary to the Holy Blessed Mother for strength and rely on prayer, knowing that one day they would be reunited with him.

That week led into the following months and years of sorrow in missing Walter.

Their father finally found work as a sanitation engineer with the city, better known as a garbage man. He would work the trucks that picked up garbage outside of every home on the streets assigned to the truck. The truck had a three-man crew—a driver, and two haulers. They rotated in two-hour shifts so each could get a chance to rest when another was driving.

Sometimes what people threw out was useful to others, especially to the poor. It was referred to as "mongo." As a result, nothing matched in the Lang apartment. Kitchen chairs were all different, some made of metal, others made of wood. The patterns on the chairs only matched when two or more were "acquired" at the same time. Living room furniture made it to the curbside for garbage pickup only when the stuffing was all out of the chairs and couches.

The mongo served its purpose for the Lang family when they moved from one apartment to another. Landlords would incentivize families to stay and gave them two months' free rent after the first year. So, every fourteen months, all the Lang's belongings and mongo would be moved to a new apartment. The rest of the neighborhood did the same.

The Langs stopped moving when William, Sr. retired from the Sanitation Department. He became the superintendent of 276 Prospect Park West and his pay was free rent.

4 ENLISTING IN THE MILITARY

As Billy grew in age, he along with many men in the Park Slope neighborhood and who were of the acceptable age were being drafted to enlist in the Armed Forces. This draft was all-inclusive—if you did not have a legitimate reason to be deferred, then you were drafted.

These young men could be assigned to any branch of the service that was next in line to receive reinforcements. For example, if the Navy lost ten ships and their personnel had to be replaced for the new ships, draftees went into the Navy.

There were incentives for going into the Navy. The Brooklyn Navy Yards, where five ships at a time were being built, had Navy personnel running the place. If you had any experience in metallurgy, electrical or welding you could almost be assured that you would spend your enlistment in Downtown Brooklyn. Coming home at night to sleep on the weekends with the cot on the base for the weekdays was a plum assignment for those in the neighborhood. Of course, one could have been assigned to Norfolk Virginia where ships were also being built.

Billy's brother, Joe, went to the enlistment office six months before Billy did and was assigned to the Army Air Corps where he was a crewman on B-17 long-range bombers. His job was to man heavy defensive armament as a door gunner.

Joe, during his service, met up with his best friend Lefty Niemeyer completely by chance in England. The story recounted was that Lefty got so drunk, that he passed out. Joe and his friends put him on their aircraft which was assigned to move troops from England to a base in France, closer to the battle lines. Lefty was very surprised when he woke up in France the morning after he was due to be on duty in England.

As for Billy, he realized it was close to his draft time and he decided to sign up for the Army in 1943. Three weeks after he signed up, in

the middle of the summer, he was bussed down to Louisiana . There he completed his basic training and testing.

The Army assigned him as a scout. He was responsible to go before the troops and find the enemy. He was taught how to do a quick assessment of the enemy and report back to command, then figure out the best way to attack and kill the enemy.

Billy would recount later in life that Louisiana had bugs as big as Brooklyn rats and the drill instructors were Southerners still fighting the Civil War. It is there he learned how to detest second lieutenants who themselves were miserable because their rank made them salute everyone. They saluted all the officers above their rank and returned salutes to everyone below their rank. The only personnel they did not have to salute were people of the same rank. However, they saluted each other anyway to be on the safe side.

After six weeks of training as a scout or forward observer, Billy was given thirty days leave with orders to report to a transport ship in the Brooklyn Navy Yard for deployment to fight the Germans in Europe.

Billy said goodbye to his parents and siblings from the deck of an English troop carrier.

The old English cruise ship for those three weeks was converted to a troop transport. The ship joined a flotilla that included destroyers, other troop ships and hospital ships.

Billy sweated the three week trip out, where they evaded German U-boats to land safely on the docks in England.

Seventy percent of the troops were sick from either mal de mar or the hardtack and grits that they were fed. If the government knew American GIs were being transported, Billy thought, then why not feed the troops what they were used to? When he and his fellow GIs arrived in England, they were hungry and weak. They had a planned three-week period for equipment retooling and clothing change to winter garb.

Unfortunately, Billy and other scouts were given just one week as they were needed on the front lines to replace the scouts who were killed, wounded or captured.

5 MESSAGES HOME

After he left for Louisiana, Billy promised his mother that he would write home regularly. He didn't have a steady girlfriend as he didn't want the attachment to be something he had to worry about.

His mother and father got only two letters from him that were personally written before he ended up in enemy hands.

One was from Louisiana, when he was on a break from training. The second letter they received was written from the transport ship detailing his misery with the food, ship, sleeping arrangements, seasickness and anything else he could complain about.

Despite the lack of letters, Billy's mother Mary, on a weekly basis, gathered the family around the kitchen table to write a family letter letting Billy know that everything was fine at home—even if it wasn't. She figured he had to keep his mind focused, given the news she heard on the radio. She wasn't going to give him anything else to worry about. Besides what could he do from there? Billy was already sending home half of his pay and it was sorely needed.

After Billy landed in England, the communication stopped. Mary and the rest of the family chalked it up to an all-encompassing subject everyone was talking about—the War.

Christmas week came and that's when Mary did receive word, but not from her son. She received a telegram from Western Union. It was a message no parent whose son was serving would want to receive.

The telegram was short and to the point. Mary read the telegram a few times and even turned it over, hoping some information or instructions on what she could or should do, or who she could or should call, was on the back. Nothing was there.

*"THE SECRETARY OF WAR DESIRES TO EXPRESS HIS
DEEP REGRET THAT YOUR SON, PRIVATE WILLIAM
LANG HAS BEEN REPORTED MISSING IN ACTION SINCE
DECEMBER 14 IN BELGIUM.
IF FURTHER DETAILS OR OTHER INFORMATION BE
RECEIVED YOU WILL BE PROMPTLY NOTIFIED"*
-- THE ADJUCANT GENERAL

"At least the government expressed regret," she told others.

For months, there was no further communication on Billy. Those days and weeks were filled with fear and continued worry over his fate. They didn't know his whereabouts and neither did the U.S. Army.

The Lang family could only do for Billy what they did during tragic and trying times: They prayed for him and all the other soldiers serving and for their safe return.

A few months later, on February 1, 1945 a second telegram arrived at the Lang residence.

This one was no better than the first.

The telegram stated: *"YOUR SON HAS BEEN CAPTURED AND IS NOW A PRISONER OF WAR"*

At least he is alive! his mother thought.

Then the realization that her son was in the hands of the enemy hit her. Frustration took over at the circumstances and also because the U.S. Government could provide her with no additional information.

In mid-February, however, she received a postcard with Billy's handwriting dated December 29, 1944. His name, rank and division of the military was in his handwriting, and the camp where he was held was also written by him. All the other words on the postcard were in French. The preprinted postcard had STALAG XIII D, the name of the prison camp. The preprinted words on the postcard read:

"I am a prisoner of war in Germany and in good health. We will be transporting soon from here to another camp in a few days. Do not write just yet until you receive my new address."

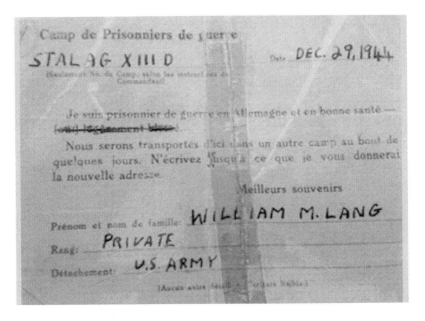

Mary, also later called Nana by her grandchildren, said she prayed constantly to the Holy Mother Mary to keep her son safe, bring all the soldiers home and the war to end quickly. Her prayers were constant as were her continual concern and fear for her son who was in the enemy's hands.

Billy would need all of his street smarts and prayers to keep him alive in the most perilous journey and trying times of his life.

The next five chapters of this book are the unedited words of Billy as he recited in tape recordings his experiences on the battlefield, his job as a scout, his capture by the Nazis, his imprisonment and his eventual escape. Billy's story in his own words were worthy of keeping these following chapters in the first person.

6 PRELUDE TO CAPTURE, DECEMBER 1944

I was sent up to the 32nd Calvary on the Luxembourg border facing the Siegfried line. We were attached to the 28th Infantry Division, called the Bloody Bucket, that suffered about 70 percent casualties before they got to Luxembourg. It was a great and proud infantry division. Most of our duties were to hold the outpost and scout the land between Luxembourg and the Siegfried line. Every morning, our patrol would go out to see if any Germans infiltrated our lines during the night.

Around December 10, 1944, we pulled back to Belgium to a rest area. We were all given complete physicals and we cleaned up our equipment and weapons. On the second day, my 32nd Calvary Recon Platoon was put on the alert to go up and relieve our other group of reconnaissance, the 18th Recon, who was getting the hell beat out of them from small pockets of Germans who were feeling out our lines. It was around December 15 when we were alerted and rushed up to action at the front.

The 106th Infantry Division had no combat experience and was made up of GIs who were learning how to be specialists in the Army. It seems that the Germans knew the weak spot to hit and they succeeded in killing a great many of our American soldiers. They fought bravely but the odds were against them.

The Germans were experienced, and they were hardened troops fighting against the 106th Infantry, 70% of which were inexperienced green call-ups. As we reached our destination we were told that we had been attached to the 106th Infantry Division.

The front was a disaster and everyone was retreating except us. No one knew what was going on, and there was mass confusion. It seemed that the rear brass was asleep or just plain stupid.

While we were in the town of Honsfeld, my company took a stand. My corporal, Private Whitey and I were ordered to go up and make contact with the enemy and report back. On our way, we tried to stop American trucks to find out what was going on. Nobody would stop, it was a full retreat. The weather was bad and the muddy roads were covered with slush.

As we got up further to a town near Auw, one last two-and-a-half-ton truck was leaving. They informed us that five Tiger tanks were a half a mile down the road, then they took off. The three of us were the only ones left up there between the Americans and the Germans.

We decided to take refuge in a barn and the Corporal told me to put the 30-caliber machine gun up in the loft of the barn. I refused because the German civilians we encountered were very amused that the Germans were coming back.

I told the Corporal that I would put the gun up there on one condition: I would shoot the civilians first since I knew they would give away our position. He looked at me like I was crazy, but I meant it. He then decided that we should leave because my 30-caliber machine gun was no match for a Tiger tank.

Moments later Whitey and I looked down the valley and saw a mass of German soldiers in white sheets coming up the hill. They wore white sheets to camouflage themselves in the snow. Our hearts leaped into our mouths as we saw the enemy was approaching.

We got the hell out of there fast.
The whole way back was mass confusion. We had only been gone a few hours and our comrades wrote us off as being dead or captured.

When we got back to our lines, all our guys had their weapons ready to shoot us. Apparently, the Germans were coming through the line in American uniforms. Lucky for us, someone recognized us and they held their fire.

We gave our officer our report that included the information about the tanks and the massive German troop movement. This information was passed on to our intelligence division.

Unfortunately, it seemed that they didn't take the situation seriously. No support was sent up and we wondered why the top brass didn't heed our warnings.

This is part of the reason why thousands of GIs were killed and captured, I believe. Later it was dubbed The Battle of the Bulge. I think a better name would have been "Bungle of the Bulge" as thousands died because our own inexperienced officers refuse to act responsibly. After observing one general's leadership skills I believe that he received his stars in a Cracker Jack Box.

7 CAPTURED BY ENEMY, CHRISTMASTIME

The night of December 15th was hell. Our outfit had orders to hold the town of Honsfeld, Belgium. Men were put on outposts in the town. We picked straws long and short to see who would go to the outposts. I had picked the straw that put me in the barn with my lieutenant. Before we got to the farm, we could hear shell fire all around the town. A sergeant, another GI and I went to the barn to get some needed rest. The sergeant got up and told me he was going to the farmhouse. I told him to wake us if anything was happening and not to forget we were in there.

I could hear tanks passing the barn all night and I also heard gunfire. I went into the farmhouse at around five or six in the morning. The old man and his family who live there told me that my comrades took off during the night. As I looked outside, all of our light tanks and Jeeps were intact so I thought they would be back. (I found out later that the SS had killed the old man and his son for harboring American GIs.)

As I checked the outside of the house and the crossroad, I saw the bodies of many GIs. They were strewn all over. Photos from the

31

National Archives would later reveal there were numerous American casualties.

I then heard shots and realized I was the target. I ran back to the barn to wake up the other GI to tell him we had been left behind.

Knowing our lives were in danger I decided to hide in the outside building that was used for storage. I buried the tall GI first then I buried myself in the debris.

As I lay there I heard Germans speaking outside and one of them came into the building and looked around for contraband. He re-entered a little while later with six or seven Germans who had burp guns. "Come out American GIs," they yelled. I did not move. I was scared to death. They pulled the debris off me and I stuck up my hand and said, "Comrades."

They took me outside and started to question me, putting an American .45 gun barrel between my eyes. I gave them my name, ranked and serial number, something we were told to give if ever captured by the enemy.

One German drew back on the barrel, cocked the trigger of the gun and pressed the barrel to my temple. I looked at the dead American GIs around me, knowing I would soon be one of them. I silently said a prayer and said to them, "I will be joining you fellas in the few moments."

The next thing I knew I was face down after taking a blow to the back of my head. I was pushed and marched to the farmhouse basement with other captured GIs. As far as I knew they did not find the other GI that I buried. I hoped he made it to safety.

In the basement, there were many men from my platoon who were also captured. They were asking me why they were left in Honsfeld. I couldn't answer them, as I was also left. About an hour later they brought the other GI that I had hidden in the debris. One German guard looked at me and smirked, knowing that I had lied. His expression told me I would pay for my silence.

That night, the Air Force bombed the hell out of the town and out of us who were there since we were still in the basement of the farmhouse. We were lucky the building did not get hit.

That was the last raid the Americans were able to perform for many days because of overcast weather.

My good friend, Chichester, who I met later in the prison camp had been in the other part of town fighting from a schoolhouse with about a dozen men. They were ordered by a German tank commander to surrender or be blasted out by the German Tiger tanks. They had no choice but to surrender as it would have been suicide not to give up. They fought like hell but had no choice with the Tiger tanks against them.

The two groups of men from the schoolhouse and farmhouse were marched off toward Germany. As we marched we were heckled by the youths of the German army and those in tanks. We were a laughingstock to them, trophies in the game of war. They took our winter gloves and clothes leaving us with field jackets and shoes that soaked up the wet snow.

Most of our toes were getting frozen as we marched for three days without food. We ate snow to quench our thirst.

The first camp we came upon to contained Russian POWs. They were very friendly and shared bread with sugar on it with us. It was the first food we had in days. We noticed that the Russian POWs were badly mistreated by the Germans—they hated each other.

I met Russian allies who said they had their legs, arms, and hands amputated without anesthetics. If you got gangrene, the other Russian GIs would hold you down while others would amputate and cauterize the infected wound. We stayed with them one night and then we were herded onto the boxcars.

8 POW CAMP XIII D NUREMBERG

It was late December, 1944, when we were marched to the train station and put into a boxcar, crowded in so much that we were all standing. Everyone was hungry and we all had diarrhea. We had not eaten anything for three days except for what the Russians had fed us.

For two days we traveled in the feces drenched boxcar. Men were using their helmets as makeshift toilets. When we stopped one day by a river, we cleaned out the helmets.

Some men drank water from the river as they were so thirsty, but that didn't help their malnutrition and constant diarrhea caused by dysentery. It was December 25th, Christmas Day, and we spent it in a boxcar.

I was depressed beyond measure. All I could think of were my parents, brothers and sisters celebrating in a warm home with good food on the table. I was hoping that they didn't receive any telegrams indicating that I was missing.

As bad as we had in the hell of that boxcar, we did manage to sing a few Christmas carols. It helped us forget, for a few moments, the hell we were experiencing and the uncertainty that lay ahead of us. One song really hit home for me:

"Silent night, holy night

All is calm, all is bright

Round yon Virgin Mother and Child

Holy Infant so tender and mild

Sleep in heavenly peace

Sleep in heavenly peace…"

As we reached our destination some men were immediately put to work on farms. I was put on the state farm owned by Herr Spatz around Nunstad. I caught pneumonia and they let stay in the cold barracks for one day. I knew if I lay there any longer I would have died, so I got out to work the next day. We stayed there for a couple of weeks and were put back into the boxcars toward Nuremberg Luftwaffe Camp XIIID.

When we arrived at Nuremberg, we were lined up in the freezing weather outside of the barracks. The officers were on one side separated from the enlisted men. One officer was telling the German guards that officers should not be treated like this. He said that the officers deserved better treatment but he didn't say anything about the enlisted men. He was a poor example of an American officer who didn't consider his men first. As much as the Germans were hated for treating us with disrespect, that officer drew the enlisted men's ire and brought us closer together.

Camp life was as close to hell as anywhere can get. Men were dying all around me from gangrene, dehydration and starvation. We were always hungry, freezing and physically and mentally exhausted. I didn't know how much more I could endure.

To keep warm men slept together on the straw mattresses. Sleeping in the barracks was like sleeping in an icebox. I had no bed pal until my good buddy, Chichester, asked me to share with him. At that moment there was a bond between two GIs that was closer than brothers. That bond lasted a lifetime.

Every morning we were forced out of the barracks with bayonets. The men who were able to walk were marched to the town of Nuremberg for forced labor. Many men had frozen feet and gangrene and could not get out of bed. Some of us had a cup of tea and the bite of bread that we would save from our main dinner of

grass soup the night before. We arrived in the mornings after we spent most nights doing nine hours of hard labor in zero degree temperatures.

We marched every day to work. We passed a large stadium with a huge swastika hanging in the front.

Aside from our bodies being pushed beyond their limits and dealing with the pain and suffering from our physical condition, our mental boundaries were also tested.

We had to dig graves and bury the dead from the American air raid bombings. It was so traumatizing. I cried for those bodies I buried and said a silent prayer for them and their families.

One day in Nuremberg I was cleaning out a bombed building. The Germans instructed us to hand over anything of value to them. I was up on the third floor and found a big clock that measured pressures. The guards were not on that floor and I picked up a large boulder and crushed it since I did not want to give it to them. I did not want the Germans to salvage anything that our flyboys missed.

What I did not realize that another GI saw me crush it, and he said he was going to tell the Germans about it. If he came in favor with the Germans they would give him extra food.

I told him something to scare the hell out of him. He stayed away from me after that and did not tell them. If he had told them, I would have been shot for the act.

In the prisoner of war camp, Chi and I were always together. We gathered twigs and branches on the way back to the camp to try to heat the barracks. The Germans only gave us only four chunks of coal a day for heat which was far less than we needed in the cold temperatures.

We were only given one Red Cross package to share with four GIs. If the package contained cigarettes they were very valuable. We could trade them for bread with the German citizens. It helped us survive a little longer. I saw GIs trade their food for cigarettes and later starve to death.

Three weeks before we left Nuremberg Camp the Germans moved a group of captured Air Force men next to us. We were separated by barbed wire and dogs. It seemed they were treated pretty well by the Luftwaffe. They had plenty of Red Cross packages, but the Germans would not let any of them throw food or other goodies over the fence to us.

Chi and I saw the good stuff on the other side and we decided to crawl over there after dark. While the dogs were at the other end of the compound we got through the barbed wire to the Air Force barracks. They gave us a lot of goodies.

About 10 p.m. we started to head back but the air raid sirens went off and all the guards were out in full force. We had to wait until about 4 a.m. when all was quiet.

With the help of a prayer, we made it back to our barracks without getting shot.

Life in the prison camp for all of us was about the same. We were all underfed and full of lice. Most of the time I felt that it might have been more merciful to be killed since we were living towards a slow death anyway. But the life that we had in us kept us going. We also felt and hoped that the war wouldn't last much longer.

While working one day two GIs on work detail had passed an SS office and took a couple of cookies off a desk. They were caught, taken away and executed.

9 OUR ESCAPE FROM THE NAZIS

As the fighting was getting close to us we were told that we were getting shipped out to the north. That day a few thousand GIs and I marched to be put in boxcars again for another journey. With us was another prisoner, Richard Goose Castleberry. We were left in the railroad yard that night, our enemy hoping that we would be bombed by our own forces.

We learned later that intelligence was informed that we were there. The next morning, we left the railroad yard and traveled for about a day, and the bombers attacked the rail yard the following night.

At the next camp we were taken to we were given an extra ration of bread and forced to march with about 2,000 men headed north. We marched all morning.

Physically and mentally exhausted, we didn't know where we were headed. That afternoon, I told Chi and Goose that we should escape the line of prisoners because I had a feeling that the end of the war was near. We all agreed to take the chance because we didn't know if the Germans were taking us on our death march.

As history later proved a great many GIs wound up in Russia and were never seen alive again. Our allies were no better than the enemy.

The three of us had a plan. We would duck, one by one, into the bushes when we reached the next curve or bend in the road. We noticed that the German guards were out of sight for a moment when the roads turned sharply. The three of us saw our opportunity and took it at the same time. We lay in the bushes for an hour waiting until the road was clear.

We then had to cross to the other side of the road. I told Chi and Goose that I would go over first and if I didn't signal them they should run the other way. When I reached the other side it was clear, so we started our journey to the American lines. With nothing to eat but a few slices of bread, we headed west.

The first day wasn't that easy. Every way we went and neared a town, we would have to backtrack because the German civilians would chase us. Our feet were swollen from frostbite as we walked in the snow over mountains. Our tired bodies were just exhausted and constantly hungry. Goose was six-foot-two and was the worse of the three of us. Chi and I were in a little better shape.

Chi was very encouraging to us both. He had a way of making our suffering a little less painful and kept convincing us we had to keep going. We marched all day and tried to rest a little at night, but we were freezing and could not sleep because we knew we might not wake up.

The second day was about the same. We dodged many German troops and had to double back many times. It seems that we had a long way to go and our hunger and frozen bodies would not handle much more. Somehow as the day passed, we managed to keep going. The third day was hell. Goose told us he could no longer go on and he wanted to surrender to the Germans. We talked to him a long time and could not persuade him to keep going.

Chi and I were forced to leave Goose, who looked so downtrodden, sitting on a bolder. Chi and I felt bad about leaving him, but we knew we had to keep going and there was no convincing him.

We hiked around a mountain and after three hours we came upon Goose, sitting on a boulder. We asked him how he got there so fast. He said he hadn't moved.

We were reunited unexpectedly and hugged. Until this day I think God steered us back so we could be together again. Some lead scout I turned out to be, I thought to myself.

Now that Goose was rested, we continued on together. It was getting dark when we came upon a farm with a barn in the distance. We decided that we would seek shelter there for the night.

As we crossed the field, we picked up frozen potatoes and turnips and put them in our pockets, eating some to fill our empty stomachs. We found the barn was empty and went up into a nice straw loft. Like happy pigs on the farm, we were finally going to get a good night's sleep with food in our stomachs.

We were dozing off, and we heard the door under the loft open. A Tiger Tank pulled into the barn. Did we not learn anything about barns? We didn't dare move. All night long we heard the Germans talking below us. Thank God they didn't come up to the loft. Tiger Tank crews took no prisoners. They would have killed us on the spot. They rolled out at daybreak and about half an hour later so did we. We ran towards the woods and kept going. We traveled pretty far and past a lot of German troops and towns.

After traveling all that day, we came upon a stone quarry. There was a little shack with a potbelly stove. It was getting dark, and we we very tired and cold. We decided that we would burn the wood and cook the potatoes and turnips that we had taken from the farm.

The fire was nice and warm and the cooked mickeys tasted great. It was the first hot meal we had in a long time. We had a fine place for lodging that night except for the German rockets which frequently flew overhead. We had no idea what was happening. The next morning all was quiet. We looked outside and spotted a young German soldier. He yelled, "Americans!" We said we were workers, and he ran away like hell. Gunfire and bombs could be heard in the distance. Goose and I decided to go down the hill and search around.

We found a bivouac shelter with numerous German knapsacks scattered all over. We got a lot of bread from them and went back to the shack to tell Chi what we found: The Germans had run.

10 SIGHT OF ANGELS

After a while, Chi and Goose went back down the hill and I could hear them yelling for me to come down. When I joined them, the three of us saw the advancing columns of American infantry marching up the road. We felt so proud of them. They look like angels to us. At long last, our ordeal came to an end and we were with our own army.

As we marched together into the next town the GIs gave us some salami, bread and anything else they had. We ate a lot and that night we got deathly ill, vomiting until our stomachs were empty. Our bodies were unaccustomed to eating so much.

We were sent back by Jeep towards an airfield. Our clothes were rags and we looked terrible. An officer saw us and said we were a disgrace. I didn't know what he expected us to look like after months of hell!

We were flown back to France to Camp Lucky Strike where we were deloused and given new clothes. A few days later, we were sent home on a hospital ship. We arrived at Camp Dix in New Jersey on May 6, and two days later we were each on our way home for a month's furlough.

Chi, Goose and I were so excited we did not get each other's addresses. We lost contact, however the story of Chi and I did not end here.

11 BILLY RETURNS HOME

They noticed he was moody, withdrawn and quick to anger. Others eyed him with suspicion. How could anyone come through that ordeal without some mental deficiencies?

What happened at that POW Camp, what did he see, what did they do to him?

Billy felt people eyeing him and treating him differently, and he felt that no one would understand what he went through. Bringing up his hellish experience would only make him relive it.

So he took his experiences and buried them deep down inside. It would remain there until much later in his life when he was made to confront his demons by seeing a psychiatrist from the Veteran's Administration.

Settling back into a civilian life, he got a job as a carpenter's apprentice. It was an entry position with the carpentry union which was hiring veterans with honorable discharges. He also had to know someone as a sponsor in order to work in that capacity. One of his friends who had worked his way up to a master carpenter position during the war knew that Billy was dependable and recommended him.

He started dating again and found a girl he grew serious with. They were set up by mutual friends. Her name was Mary and on the walk home they held hands and kissed when they said good night to each other.

Billy really liked being with her especially because she didn't ask questions about the war. Mary heard from others that he was a POW and figured that in time he would come around to talking about it. She instinctively felt that this was the man with whom she could spend her life.

After four months, Billy and Mary began to think about marriage. Life was again slowly starting to make sense and he was relatively happy. They would talk to each other daily and she was so proud to be with him. Arm in arm they would walk through Prospect Park, stopping every once in a while to make out. Those in the neighborhood assumed this couple would finally be engaged and married.

Billy's mother met her and she was impressed and liked her. After all, her oldest son Joe was to be married within six months and she thought her second son was certainly of age. Her husband was oblivious to such things and trusted his wife with the intuition for such matters.

Mary then started to become sick. Billy noticed that she had lost a lot of weight and energy. She took a day off to go to the doctors, and blood work revealed she had leukemia.

It was a death sentence.

Six weeks from when she was diagnosed, Mary passed away. Billy was beside himself, questioning why this woman he finally met after so much misery in his life had to leave him.

Love never dies, Billy knew, and he would carry his love for Mary for the rest of his life.

12 LOVES LOST AND FOUND

Tragedy again hit home for Billy and his family on a Wednesday afternoon, May 22, 1946. His brother, Eddie, and a friend were sitting in the bosses' office in a small bed spring manufacturing plant. They decided to look into the desk and there they found a 9-shot Russian revolver. They started playing with it. Whether this was a game of Russian roulette will never be known.

The gun went off and the bullet penetrated the femoral artery in Eddie's groin. Within minutes his blood spread across the floor and Eddie asked for the Rosary beads that were in his pocket. By the time anyone in the plant could react, Eddie was already fighting to stay conscious.

He died before EMTs could arrive.

A picture was taken and the front page of the New York Daily Mirror showed a crying Eddie, staring up at the camera, with the Rosary beads wrapped around his hands.

He left behind grieving parents, six brothers, and two sisters. He was 17. Once again, Billy was forced to confront the loss of a loved one. Billy and Eddie were very close to each other as Eddie was the younger brother and Billy protected him from the streets.

Eddie's girlfriend, Rose Kennedy, quietly sobbed at the wake and funeral mass. She and Eddie weren't together that long, but his death was hard for her. At the repast, Billy was curious about what drew her and Eddie together. Billy found a very wounded and conflicted person just like himself.

13 ROSE AND BILLY BEGIN THEIR JOURNEY

Rose was born into abject poverty in Brooklyn, on August 1, 1930. Her father, James Kennedy, lost his job the year of the Great Depression and could not find steady work.

Her father would hit the bottle to forget his joblessness and his ability to feed his family and then focus his outrage on his family.

Rose and her sister Anna would hide in the closet when they saw their father coming home drunk.

The girls, dressed in ragged clothing, had a makeshift cart that they pushed and pulled through the neighborhood to collect wood to burn for heat and hot water. Sometimes they were sent to the Brooklyn Navy Yard for coal, which was miles away from their home.

Many nights, the Kennedy family had no food and the girls and their younger brothers went to bed hungry. Anne, the matriarch of the family, adopted a persona of someone with deficient mental capacities, but she was anything but dumb.

Billy's mother, Mary, was acquainted with Anne and her situation. She would buy groceries for the Kennedy family and convinced others in the neighborhood to step up and contribute.

At 15, Rose took a job at a printing office. There, she worked long hours. She and her sister worked to be away from home, and their pay would go directly to the rent and food for the family.

Rose met Eddie when she turned 16 and they dated a few months until his death.

Rose and Billy remained friends and he eventually asked her out on a date at an Italian restaurant on Fifth Avenue in Brooklyn.

The restaurant made their own wine and served it in small bottles to the customers who asked for it. The restaurant did not have a liquor license but the food was so good that the police looked the other way.

It was this girl, Rose, who won Billy's heart and they eventually fell in love. Two hearts, both in need of mending were joined and they found that together they were stronger. Rose, for the first time in her life, felt love in its purest form. It was a love she would be willing to die for.

It was a hot night in July when Billy got down on one knee at the restaurant where they had their first date and proposed to Rose. After she said yes, the patrons all applauded. The waiter served champagne to the happy couple who were married a year later on July 10, 1948.

14 HUMBLE BEGINNINGS

The first place the newly married couple occupied was a one-bedroom apartment on Flatbush Avenue and Avenue D. While living there, Rose gave birth to their first-born child, William (also called Wullum).

The apartment was very tight with one child, let alone a second child when James (also called Jamus) was born 18 months after his brother.

The family of four then moved to a three-bedroom apartment back in Park Slope, 268 Prospect Park West. This, like many other buildings, held seven families with an indeterminate number of occupants. On each side of the entrance there were two small stores. On the right side, a Chinese laundry, which was a booming business. They washed and starched all the white wash, sheets, undershirts and underpants. On the left side, one of the first pizzerias in the neighborhood opened. The price of a slice of pizza was fifteen cents and a Coke was a dime.

The Langs occupied one of the top floor apartments and its set up was peculiar. The bathtub was in the kitchen and the communal toilet bowl and sink were outside in the hallway, in the landing between two apartment front doors. When their third son Gary was born, the parents started potty training James. When a three-year-old needs to go, he really needs to go. The parents thus had a hard time training James.

Every fifteen minutes Rose would ask her son, "Do you have to go to the potty?" and most times he was okay. When he said he had to go, she'd scramble to get his pants down and diaper off, and rush him to the communal toilet. When he got into the bathroom and did potty, he was congratulated and told what a big boy he was. But most times, the communal toilet was occupied. It made for a very trying potty training lesson.

The bathtub in the kitchen was logically placed next to the hot water heater that was centered between the tub and the kitchen sink. It made for interesting bathing. Seeing that the hot water heater's capacity was only ten gallons, Billy bathed first. If he got out

at a reasonable time, in went the other children. By the time all of the children were cleaned, the water was the color of putty.

After living at that apartment for three years, the Langs packed their belongings and moved across to 17th St.

15 RAISING A DOZEN

After living at the apartment on 17th Street for fourteen months, the Langs packed their belongings and moved on up to 276 Prospect Park West.

Like the other apartments, there were three flights of stairs to trek up in order to get to the top-floor apartment. One significant difference from the other apartments was that there was a whole bathroom in its own room inside the apartment! The Lang family was living in luxury now, with their own bathtub, sink and toilet.

Timothy was the fourth child born to Rose and Billy and his arrival happened in the apartment the day after Christmas. Timothy was ready to enter into the world and couldn't wait for the ambulance to get there. Between Billy's mother, who lived in a downstairs apartment, and Rose, they both figured out how to birth the child.

When the police arrived, they saw that the old woman knew what she was doing, so they stepped back and got out of the way.

Transportation arrived shortly thereafter and Timothy and Rose were transported to Methodist Hospital for five days of rest, which was the typical rest period at the time.

Now with four children, Rose was in great shape. Dragging up and down three flights of stairs with the baby in the carriage and running after three toddlers resulted in her body being like an Olympian.

When the fifth son, Martin, was born, the three large bedrooms started looking a lot smaller. The twin beds held two children each and a crib held Marty. When Marty started climbing out of the crib, Billy put the twin beds together and the five boys slept in the same bed.

When Marty turned three, he would run up the stairs ahead of Rose. One time she got distracted and Marty reached the second floor alone. He climbed up the railing and while looking over, he fell two flights down and landed hard on the marble flooring.

Marty's head was split open across the top from one ear to the other. An ambulance was called, but the cops arrived first. With the hospital only a mile away, Rose wrapped the seizing toddler in a blanket and jumped into the back of the cop car.

With sirens blaring and lights flashing, the cops sped them to the emergency room. The doctor in the ER immediately called for X-rays and notified the head trauma specialist on call that his services were needed.

Rose went with the stretcher and into the X-ray room as Marty was having more seizures. The technician directed Rose to stay and hold him down. After three tries, he finally had a picture that showed the fracture. Back in the ER, the trauma specialist and Billy appeared to arrive at the same time.

The doctor took a look at the X-ray films and said that he needed to consult with the brain surgeon. He would have more information once the surgeon looked at the films taken, and needed to repeat the process every hour for a comparison.

Rose finally broke down, crying into her husband's shoulder. Marty was transferred to the children's ward in a room of his own. Rose went home to her other four sons and Billy stayed with Marty and as is typical in troublesome times, had his Rosary beads in hand.

The following morning, a team of doctors came into the room and woke up Billy. Marty was still in a coma. The doctor took Billy aside and told him that his son's condition was dire.

"The next few days will tell us a lot about his condition. As of an hour ago, the X-ray showed that the brain was still swelling. It has slowed down significantly but it has not stopped," the doctor told him. He also indicated that some cognitive functions could be impaired.

After the team left, Billy sat back down and put his head down to pray.

"I prayed to the Blessed Mother and to Jesus to bring Marty back as he was before the fall," he told his sons when he got home. He also told them to pray for their brother.

Billy also mentioned that he had met a nurse. She was an older woman who came into the room and saw him praying. She placed her hand on his shoulder and said, "I see a man who has a special relationship with Jesus."

The nurse told him she was retiring within the month, and there was no way she would let Marty pass on her watch. She sent Billy home to be with his wife and the rest of his children.

The next day, Billy had to go to work at his second job at he funeral parlor. After serving as pallbearer at a funeral, he picked up his wife and headed straight to the hospital.

When they entered the room, Marty was awake and alert, wearing a helmet so he would not hurt himself. By that afternoon they moved him to another room with three other patients. They changed his bed to his crib and put a netting over it so he could not get out.

The nurse who promised Marty would not die came into the room and gave Billy a big bear hug and smiled at Rose.

"He woke out of his coma this morning at 5 a.m. He said he was hungry so we got a tray from downstairs with breakfast. He ate eggs and hash browns, drank juice and asked for more," the nurse told Rose and Billy.

They all smiled, prayed, and Rose and Billy shared tears of joy. They also realized that a possible miracle occurred and thanked God for saving their son.

Marty was home within a week and still was wearing the helmet. However, it only lasted on his head for a couple of hours.

After her son's brush with death, life with five children returned to as normal as it possibly could. Rose didn't realize at the time of the accident that she was pregnant with her sixth child. She had a miscarriage a few months into her pregnancy. Rose wondered why she lost the child and felt an intense loss. Rose realized years later that the X-ray she held Marty down for may have been the cause.

A year later, Rose gave birth to her sixth son, Donald, and he was affectionately called "Duck." He arrived just when Marty was due to enter the communal twin bedroom. It was obvious that the family had outgrown the apartment, as there was little space for anyone to have any solitude.

16 MISCHIEF

Billy and Rose ended up having twelve children. For the most part, each were born eighteen months apart. Each day held a new adventure and most times with twelve children mischief would inevitably ensue.

One such story of Lang childhood mischief occurred shortly after Timothy was born.

Billy had purchased a number of gallons of white paint to try to put a fresh face on the peeling ceilings and walls in the apartment.

There was a small paint factory on 20th Street, where you could buy paint directly out the back door. The workers, most of whom were from Puerto Rico, got below minimum hourly pay and spoke little English. Their job was to mix colors in large vats of white paint and pour the product into paint cans. In those days, there were no custom colors. You got whatever color was being mixed at the time of purchase, at three dollars a gallon, cash only. The factory always had white paint available.

At the time, Wullum was five years old, Jamus was four and Gary was two. Timothy had just been born. The three older boys were always up at the crack of dawn, always a few hours before Billy and Rose and always ready for mischief-making and mayhem.

One morning, they thought they would help their father by painting the apartment. The cans were in the living room, so it was logical for them to start there.

After prying open a number of cans and spilling at least half a can on the rug, the boys began in earnest to show their ability as house painters. They painted the floor around the area rug, the rug itself (after all it was half done anyway), half the couch, the chairs, the TV set and each other.

It was oil-based paint and needed mineral spirits to clean it off. The kids looked for a ladder to attempt to paint the ceiling, but couldn't find one.

Everything they covered with the white paint looked good to them. Wullum and Jamus, keen on continuing to paint, decided to paint their brother, Gary, also nicknamed Butterball. They painted his whole body including his face, hair and the lids of his eyes. They even painted his pajamas and his diaper, and made sure to paint between his toes.

Billy, who woke up to Gary crying, believed he was viewing a very small ghost.

There were multiple utterances of "Oh my God!" and "Son of a Bitch" followed by a period of communal parental moaning.

Jamus and Wullum, trying to look penitent as they stared at their white painted feet, both pointed at each other as the one who instigated the situation. As they stood there in almost as much paint as Butterball, they hoped against all odds that the blame on one against the other would lessen the punishment. The strategy didn't work at the time that there were only four children.

However, when Billy and Rose reached the number of twelve children, they would give up caring who was at fault because there were several more children around blaming each other to avoid punishment.

Another mischievous event took place with the Lang family television. The Langs were one of the first families in the neighborhood to get a real color TV, and before that they were one of the the first to get a black and white TV and a film that turned it into color.

There was a commercial about making black and white TV into color. All one had to do was place a plastic colored film over the black and white TV screen and presto, the TV screen was color.

When the screen finally arrived, Billy installed it when he came home from work. That night, they got to watch Bonanza in color. In the show, the sky was a beautiful shade of blue with fluffy blue clouds and the horses were brown and green. The Ponderosa never looked as gorgeous. Hoss, Little Joe and Adam had green faces, but the Lang family didn't care. They had color TV. That was until the colored film started peeling off and bubbling up. After two weeks, Billy taped the corners and flattened out the bubbles to make it work again.

When the black and white TV with the screen was finally exhausted, Billy then bought an RCA color television, new technology at the time. It got delivered later in the day on Friday, but Billy wasn't able to install it on that particular day.

The next day, Jamus, Gary and Timothy, who were up early again, figured they help get rid of the old black white TV. They punched holes in the speakers, pulled out wires, and destroyed it. What the boys didn't know was that the old set was a down payment for the new TV. Their punishment was no television for a week.

The no TV punishment did not end the mischief. When the Langs finally were able to get new furniture for the first time, that proved to be short-lived.

Billy and Rose purchased tool kits one Christmas for their older sons, figuring it was an opportunity for them to learn the skills of using tools such as hammers, saws and screwdrivers.

They realized their mistake shortly thereafter.

One morning when their sons woke up early again, they sawed off the legs from the brand-new couches and the coffee and the end tables. They were proud of the job, until Rose and Billy awoke and screamed at their sons' handiwork.

Despite the mischief, typical of young boys, Billy and Rose loved their children and would introduce a different addition to the family of all male children, a daughter.

17 BILLY'S FIRST HOME, DAUGHTER

In 1959, Rose and Billy had their seventh child and it was finally a girl! They named her Rosanne. Unfortunately, they outgrew the 276 Prospect Park West apartment and they had nowhere to put their precious daughter.

Billy and Rose started looking for a place of their own to buy. They found a fixer-upper for $5,000 on 19th Street. Billy took a GI loan of $3,000 and borrowed the remaining money from Pete Smith, the owner of the funeral parlor where he worked his second job. They agreed Billy would work for free until the loan was paid off. It took decades to pay back Pete in labor.

A first look at the house showed it wasn't in such bad shape. It was a two-family apartment and Billy planned on reworking it into a single-family home for their growing family. The re-work on the house was substantial.

Billy made plans and enlisted workers he did not have to pay to start demolition. He made the house livable for his family and over the years did more home improvement projects.

As a new homeowner, Billy searched for advice on a number of things with respect to home ownership. One of which was how much coal to order for the upcoming winter. He sought out the superintendent of the public school on Prospect Avenue (PS 10), who advised Billy to purchase the larger chunks of coal and to order ten tons.

When the coal delivery came, Wullum was there to accept delivery. He told the coal deliverer to put the coal in the basement. Unfortunately, after filling the entire basement, another ton and a half of coal needed to be placed somewhere. Wullum chose to put the coal in the front yard.

It took an entire winter to clear the front yard of the coal, which the neighbors did not appreciate. But everyone in the house agreed it was the warmest winter they had every experienced.

As for the house with the expanding family, the five bedrooms upstairs fit the two adults and seven children
nicely. Being the only girl, Rosanne had her own bedroom. It started getting crowded again when Matthew, Gerard and Richard joined the family.

A reintroduction of pushing beds together to accommodate multiple sleepers was necessary and performed.

Richard's birth found Rose on the third page of the New York Daily News when she was caught smoking in Methodist Hospital. With no money to pay the summons, Billy told the media: "Frankly, I don't have any money to pay the summons. If they want to put her in jail, they'll have to make room for the kids too."

Cig Gives Her Pack of Trouble
Mother Tagged for Smoking in Hospital

By WILLIAM NEUGEBAUER

Speaking of his wife, newly delivered of her 10th child, William Lang, 38, said yesterday: "Frankly, I don't have any money to pay the summons. If they want to put her in jail, they'll have to make room for the kids too."

Smoking a cigaret had brought this crisis into the life of William and his wife Rose, 33, of 396 19th St., Brooklyn.

William is doing a slow burn, but it wasn't he who smoked that cigaret. He's a non-nicotine man. His wife was the one.

Her 7th Child There

She was, at the time, Friday afternoon, lying in bed in a third-floor maternity ward of Methodist Hospital, Brooklyn. Two days earlier, she had given birth to 6-pound, 10-ounce Richard Patrick Lang, her seventh child delivered in that hospital. Now she was having a meditative cigaret.

Suddenly a Fire Department inspector appeared and gave her a summons for smoking in a restricted area.

The summons is answerable Feb. 10 in Brooklyn Criminal court.

Smoking in hospitals here was restricted after the Hartford hospital fire of Dec. 8, 1961, in which 16 persons died. But Lang declared that in spite of this, hospital workers give out ash trays and demanded—

"If you're not supposed to smoke, why do they pass out ash trays?"

Explanation Given

A spokesman to whom THE NEWS passed on this question explained that there are designated smoking areas and nurses are allowed to give ash trays to visitors in these areas. Unofficially when a nurse finds a visitor smoking illegally, she may bring an ash tray so he can stub out his cigaret.

"My wife was stunned by all this," said Lang. "She's been here so many times and was never even warned before."

Lang takes home $95 a week from his job as a subway conductor, and bolsters his income by parttime work as a pallbearer.

(NEWS foto by Nick Sorrentino)
Mrs. Rose Lang, an ash band, sits in hospital.

The last two children to Billy and Rose were girls, Donna and Mary Lou, number eleven and twelve of the siblings. After the birth of Mary Lou, the doctor suggested and performed a hysterectomy on Rose.

As the youngest grew, the oldest, Wullum would leave for the U.S. Air Force in 1967 and serve in the Vietnam War. He would follow in Billy's footsteps, serving his country and protecting its freedom.

18 THE POST

Billy never talked about his war experiences. Then again, no veterans in the local Veteran's of Foreign Wars Post did either. McFadden Brothers Post 1380 memorialized two brothers who were killed in Europe during World War II.

The post opened in 1948 with nearly 300 members, called Legionnaires. Anyone who served in the military could join as a member. At the time of its formation it did not exclude noncombat veterans. It was governed by national bylaws, and each post could add laws pursuant to their particular post, as long as the national bylaws were not affected. The commander-in-chief, a co-commander, treasurer, houseman and secretary were voted on each year. Rarely, the position of commander-in- chief would be filled by the same member.

On the lower floor of the post, members gained access by going through a tunnel and knocking on the door. On that floor was a horseshoe shaped bar and the bartender worked both sides to serve the patrons. The middle of the bar housed all the liquor bottles.

There were four taps for barreled beer on the closed-end of the bar. They served Rheingold, Schaefer, Budweiser and Pabst beer. The post always had someone drinking there because the price of the beer and liquor to the patrons was subsidized by the membership. These prices were the lowest in the neighborhood.

The whole second floor on the street level was the hall. It had a capacity of 250 occupants, and could be rented by members for any occasion. Weddings, repasts and large meetings of any kind were booked well in advance. They had long tables that sat up to 12 people and the number of chairs to meet capacity. A small bar and a piano was there for liquor and entertainment. The top floor space was unusable as a meeting place because it was mostly used for storage.

Every Memorial Day the post members would march from the post hall to Holy Name Church for a special mass. Hundreds of veterans and their families attended the noon mass that was typically standing room only. After mass, the assemblage would gather at the front of the church to place a wreath at the foot of the white crucified Christ that was displayed outside the red brick church.

The priest would say a short prayer followed by a four-gun salute of blanks too loud for most of the attendees, causing them to flinch. The parade would form up once more and march to the Baptist Church on Eighth Avenue and to the synagogue where the rabbi would meet the marchers and where wreaths were laid. The assemblage would march back to the post using Prospect Park West, being applauded by the people lining both sides of Eighth Avenue. That's when the party really got started.

When the Memorial Day parade was first established it drew many veterans back to their experiences. Most of the men who came back from the war would tell you that the real heroes were the ones that were left behind. They didn't talk about politics or the reason that they were sent. Like many Americans of that time, they stayed in the neighborhood where they were born and raised, prayed on their knees every morning and evening and worked a job or jobs that were just enough for their families to get by.

The Park Slope neighborhood knew that Billy had been missing and then captured. On Memorial Day the other members would nod at him as if to say, "Yeah, I know, but now it's all right." The problem was no one knew what he went through, and that it would never be right.

Billy along with other captured soldiers experienced freezing environments and hunger to the point of starvation. They also slept in barracks that were like iceboxes as they had no heat. That forced the captured men to sleep together so they could share their body heat because they were given wafer-thin blankets.

The Nazis woke them at sunrise, fed them each a small slice of bread, marched them to clean out bombed sites by burying the bodies they found there. They were worked to the point of exhaustion. They were fed grass soup for dinner and the Nazis gave them a horse's head to add protein to the soup that the prisoners were pleased to have. Broken down brave men who had been through multiple battles to the point where those men would crawl through the rafters to steal another man's bread. No, it would never be all right.

19 POST TRAUMATIC STRESS SYNDROME

As the years went on, Billy retired from the New York Transit Authority where he worked as a conductor. That and two other jobs he worked fed his family. He also prepared tax returns for close family and friends. Since he had too many children and couldn't claim them all as dependents, he would give the others a dependent or two on their taxes.

Even though he worked three jobs, he would always say that Rose had the hardest job of all: Raising the children.

He got a job at the publishing company Ziff-Davis and retired from there after several years. He received a small pension from the company and for the first time in his life, he finally felt financially secure. A few months prior he was awarded 100% compensation by the VA. He had been getting half of that for his heart problems and frostbitten feet. The compensation addition was granted for PTSD. His net income would more than suffice, for both Rose and himself, to live a more comfortable life.

To secure a rating for PTSD, Billy would have to supply all the evidence to the VA. In order to do this, he had to first show that he has PTSD and, provide the stressor, which was that particular experience or dangerous event that caused the symptoms. He sent away for his records and discovered that they were destroyed in a fire in St. Louis in 1973. He had to use alternate resources to prove he was even in the Army!

As he was doing his research he found himself showing signs of stress. He was having nightmares of the camps all over again, interrupting his and Rose's sleep. Loud noises made him jumpy and he was exhibiting fight or flight behavior in various circumstances. These were all signs of PTSD.

Perhaps the worst symptoms were when he drank. He could never get enough and he became a belligerent drunk, which was totally out of character for him. All of his children were out of the house at this time and Rose reached out to the older siblings for help. Both Jamus and Wullum conferred and agreed that Rose would have to wait until Billy asked for help. The only time the subject should be brought up with him is when he was relatively sober. Bringing it up when he was drunk would only make matters worse.

He kept sober and busy by doing things around the house, which were projects that he never had time to do while working. He wallpapered the kitchen and put up wainscoting and a chair rail on the kitchen walls. Billy painted all the ceilings and walls where it was needed. Each day he worked, he would stop at 5 p.m. to have dinner and then he would head up to his brother Gerard's bar or the McFadden Post for a few drinks. As always Rose would wait up for him to come home before closing her eyes.

This routine would last only until there was work on the house to be done. He could justify being at the bars by telling himself that he could use a drink after he worked all day. He would still do the work at the funeral parlor even though he didn't need the money. It was just to stay busy.

His case with the VA took a turn when his advocate from the Disabled American Veterans (DAV) called to tell him that the National Jewish Welfare Board kept records on Prisoners Of War (POWs).

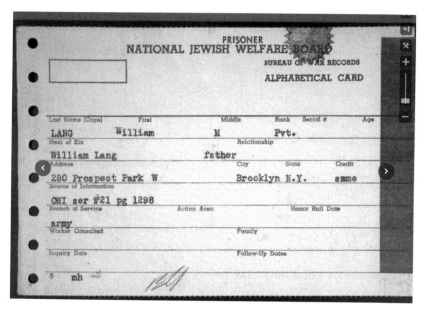

In their archives a record showed that William M. Lang was a private in the US Army and a POW. The record would not stand scrutiny if not for the fact it listed his father's name and the address of his apartment in Brooklyn.

Even given the discovery of the proof of Billy's military service and the fact that he was a POW did not seem to make a difference in his drinking habits. Flashbacks began haunting his dreams at night. He was drinking heavily, more than a quart of scotch a day. He talked to his beloved Rose, who pleaded with him to seek help.

Rose would go out with Billy on occasions, mostly to the post, where women felt more comfortable. She was drinking with him and when she felt that he had enough, she would begin the exit by saying she wanted to leave. The only problem was that she would be saying it every 15 minutes and over and over. Reluctantly he came home with her only to continue drinking there. He started telling her that he wanted to die. She in turn would tell him to seek help, knowing that he wouldn't go unless he admitted his behavior was fueled by alcohol.

Then one day in early afternoon, he began violently shaking after hearing that his close friend Charlie McLaughlin had passed. Rose covered him in blankets and when the shaking did not stop he finally conceded that he needed help. Billy checked himself into the VA hospital, diagnosed with severe depression and alcoholism.

There, he saw a psychiatrist on a regular basis and he received the tools that he needed, to remain sober. Billy was told he had a choice: "You're at a fork in the road," Mary K. from the VA told him. "You can continue on this path, or you can choose the other path."

Billy then made his decision and prayed to God for the courage to choose the sobriety path. There was a time when his faith saved him from the horrors of the camps and at this point he needed his faith to save him from an addiction he used to forget the war and its demons. He never realized that alcoholism was an addiction and he was an alcoholic.

Praying to Jesus and his Blessed Mother would help him to combat those cravings and move forward on the road to recovery. He was told that one drink would put him back to the time before he was seeking recovery.

After 45 days of rehab he was finally clean and sober. The recidivism rate for this affliction is extremely high. His immediate family were all informed and made sure he had the best chance possible of beating this disease. Rose stopped drinking to help him in his sobriety.

As for the depression, he would continue to see therapists and psychiatric help on alternating schedules in bi-monthly appointments until he felt secure enough to lengthen the time between appointments. He resigned himself to the fact that he may be seeking help for his depression for perhaps the rest of his life.

Billy stopped his drinking cold. No longer would he be a slave to alcohol and he was certain that he could prevent anyone in his family from becoming an alcoholic. He began by speaking at Alcoholics Anonymous meetings, pouring out his experiences and lending his expertise to younger men and women so they had the benefit of knowing it could be beaten.

Billy was a testament to his own iron will and a great role model for those in his family and anyone who had fallen into alcoholism or drug addiction. Upon his death, Billy was clean and sober for more than 35 years.

20 A CHALLENGE TO DRINK

Billy's faith brought him through a severe challenge and he was tempted to hit the bottle when he received a call in the summer of 1989 that his oldest son, Wullum, was in critical condition at Bellevue Hospital.

Wullum, aged 40, had taken his family out on his boat, docking it at Breezy Point. They enjoyed the day visiting with family and friends, and he was with his wife, Paula, and three of their four children. The wind picked up in the early afternoon so they decided to leave early. The boat was moored off a pier. He took off his shirt and sandals, handed them to Paula, put the boat key around his neck and jumped into the water. A submerged board that Wullum struck head-on compressed fractured his cervical spine.

He was face down in the water, unable to move and call for help. His brother, Marty, and his son, Brendan, and family members were on the pier. Marty, who thought Wullum was joking and doing the dead man's float, realized after several minutes something was wrong.

He and Brendan pulled Wullum's body to shore and began to resuscitate his non-breathing body swollen with sea water. A trauma doctor was nearby and they were able to restore breathing until help arrived.

Wullum was paralyzed from the neck down.

He was transferred to Bellevue Hospital trauma unit, then to ICU where he could have visitors. He was a sight to behold: intubated, breathing on a machine with tubes running from multiple IVs. Bags via tubes collected his urine and his feces. He refused to see his daughters looking that way, so there was motivation to begin getting his life back as much as he could.

Standing guard outside Wullum's room, Billy refused to let anyone enter until they could gather themselves. Wullum had many friends and coworkers, all of whom wanted to pay their respects. Billy told them all not to cry in front of his son. Still, there were a few who could not help themselves.

He would remain in a wheelchair for the rest of his life, the doctors predicted, but perhaps may be able to regain some upper motor skills.

The best chance for rehabilitation for their oldest son was in Colorado at Craig Hospital that specialized in rehabilitation of spinal cord injuries.

Wullum and Paula had four children. Billy and Rose decided to temporarily move to Colorado to be there for their son as he faced the most challenging time—on a physical, emotional and spiritual level—of his life.

His son's injury tested Billy's ability to remain sober.

"If there's ever a time I need a drink, it's now," Billy told Wullum, as he lay in a hospital bed with a halo brace on, unable to speak.

After six weeks in Bellevue Hospital, Wullum was flown to Craig Hospital and Billy and Rose took an apartment and they would remain with him for four months there during his rehab.

They would visit Wullum every day after his workouts and give him the courage he needed to go on. Billy never touched a drink, though he was tempted to after seeing his son with a life-changing injury and confined to a wheelchair.

21 JESUS WAS HIS BEST FRIEND

Even though one chapter probably isn't enough to describe Billy's relationship with Jesus, it is necessary to try to describe it for readers and detail what great influence religion had on his life.

Every aspect of his life reverted back to "What would Jesus do?" Every decision in his life, he prayed to God for an answer.

This isn't to say that Billy didn't stray at times. Like everyone, he was an imperfect person, but his faith is what always led him to the right road when there was the proverbial fork in it—or he picked the wrong road for an intermittent period.

Looking back, without God in his life, he would not have been able to survive all the tragedies he experienced along life's journey. Moreover, he definitely would not have been able to survive the months of hell in the Nazi prison camp.

As an example, Billy saw pure evil in the Nazi officers. One encounter in particular was when the officers tried to shake his faith. One of the officers ripped his Miraculous Medal necklace off his neck that he wore since his First Holy Communion. This was so egregious and heartbreaking to Billy that being beaten in the prison camp was more tolerable than that despicable act.

Another way that God was evident in Billy's life was through his family. Whenever one of his children would ask him advice, and the answer wasn't so clear-cut, he would tell us to pray to God for an answer. He also indicated that sometimes God doesn't answer our prayers in our time and he explained that sometimes we have to wait until he thinks we are ready.

Though that was not the answer many would like, it was something that his children learned to be true. Sometimes God's answer was, "Wait."

Aside from going to mass on Sundays, after Billy retired he and Rose and Billy attended mass every day. This wasn't a gesture to show they were holy rollers. No, it was quite the opposite. They actually wanted to go to mass. They enjoyed going every day to have that bond and closeness to God that many people work toward and perhaps few achieve in their lifetimes.

Billy would also say his Rosary daily and talk to Jesus throughout the day.

His relationship with Jesus could best be described as best friends. In fact, this is what someone once said to me: "Your father's best friend is Jesus. I've never met anyone who speaks to Jesus as if he was such a good friend."

After hearing that description, it was one that fit perfectly.

To know Billy was to know Jesus. Nearly everyone who met him or crossed his path not only respected him but revered him. He touched their lives and they were so honored and blessed to meet him.

Whether one met him for a brief encounter, knew him for years, or lucky enough to know him his entire life, it was clear to all that Billy was a special and spiritual person. You only needed to look into his eyes to see the Holy Spirit.

One priest, Father Carlos, who served in St. Mary's Mother of God church in Middletown, N.J., was one who saw the grace of God in both Billy and Rose. They became very close to Carlos and it was a relationship that lasted to the end of their lives.

Carlos saw in Billy the embodiment of God, and his homily at Billy's funeral mass described what a special man he was who did God's work on Earth.

"Billy was a true man of God," Carlos said. "He fed the poor and clothed the naked," were some words used in his homily.

Carlos went on to describe how Billy and Rose, whenever he returned to his home country of Columbia, would give him a check to spend on the poor in his hometown.

Carlos described how priests in his hometown had no vestments nor a chalice to celebrate Catholic mass.

Billy and Rose provided those items, too, to priests they didn't know so far away so mass could give comfort to those in that country. A chalice at his church was inscribed with the names of Billy and Rose and used in daily mass there.

22 BILLY REUNITED WITH CHI

It was not until 1990, at the suggestion of his VA psychiatrist who was treating Billy for PTSD, that he join a POW Post. The nearest one was in upstate New York. As part of his therapy, it was suggested that he try and bond with other people who had shared experiences as a POW and suffered from PTSD. He applied for new membership with this group by answering a post in a POW magazine.

Billy received a remarkable letter from another veteran about Nuremberg and the POW camp. That letter inquired if he was at Nuremberg Stalag XIIID   The letter was from Chichester and the two found each other 43 years later. Billy finally found the man who survived the most deplorable experiences and who was in his thoughts each day.

Billy and Chi spoke on the phone, and they made arrangements for Billy and Rose to fly to upstate New York for a meeting. Rose had trepidations about the meeting. Most times, ex-POWs did not live well. In Rose's experience, they tended towards alcoholism, psychotic episodes, drug addiction and worse. Her brother, Joe Kennedy, an ex-POW from the Korean War committed suicide a few years prior to this meeting.

Chi, his wife, Angie and his oldest son, Don, were waiting in the terminal to meet Billy and Rose. It was as if time had not passed.

The two men embraced and broke down crying into each other's arms, 43 years to the day (VE Day) when they last saw each other.

They had a remarkable reunion.

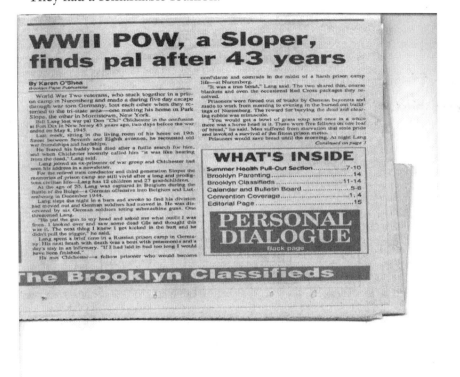

WWII POW, a Sloper, finds pal after 43 years

By Karen O'Shea
Brooklyn Paper Publications

World War Two veterans, who stuck together in a prison camp in Nuremberg and made a daring five day escape through war torn Germany, lost each other when they returned to the tri-state area—one making his home in Park Slope, the other in Morristown, New Jersey.

Bill Lang lost war pal Don "Chi" Chichester in the confusion at Fort Dix in New Jersey 43 years ago, two days before the war ended on May 8, 1945.

Last week, sitting in the living room of his house on 19th Street between Seventh and Eighth avenues, he recounted old war friendships and hardships.

He feared his buddy had died after a futile search for him, and when Chichester recently called him "it was like hearing from the dead," Lang said.

Lang joined an ex-prisoner of war group and Chichester had seen his address in a newsletter.

For the retired train conductor and third generation Sloper the memories of prison camp are still vivid after a long and prodigious civilian life—Lang has 12 children and 27 grandchildren.

At the age of 20, Lang was captured in Belgium during the Battle of the Bulge—a German offensive into Belgium and Luxembourg in December 1944.

Lang says the night in a barn and awoke to find his division had moved out and German soldiers had moved in. He was discovered by six German soldiers toting submachine guns. One threatened Lang.

"He put the gun to my head and asked me what outfit I was from. I looked over and saw some dead GIs and thought this was it. The next thing I knew I got kicked in the butt and he didn't pull the trigger," he said.

Lang spent a brief time in a Russian prison camp in Germany. His next brush with death was a bout with pneumonia and a day's stay in an infirmary. "If I had laid in bed too long I would have been finished."

He met Chichester—a fellow prisoner who would become

confidante and comrade in the midst of a harsh prison camp life—at Nuremberg.

"It was a true bond," Lang said. The two shared thin, coarse blankets and even the occasional Red Cross packages they received.

Prisoners were forced out of bunks by German bayonets and made to work from morning to evening in the burned out buildings of Nuremberg. The reward for burying the dead and clearing rubble was minuscule.

"You would get a bowl of grass soup and once in a while there was a horse head in it. There were five fellows on one loaf of bread," he said. Men suffered from starvation that stole pride and invoked a survival of the fittest prison motto.

Prisoners would save bread until the morning. At night Lang

Continued on page 3

WHAT'S INSIDE

Summer Health Pull-Out Section 7-10
Brooklyn Parenting 14
Brooklyn Classifieds 11-14
Calendar and Bulletin Board 5-6
Convention Coverage 1, 4
Editorial Page 15

PERSONAL DIALOGUE
Back page

The Brooklyn Classifieds

Chi was a teacher and coach for 30 years in the Mount Morris, New York school system. He was known in his town as Coach Chi. Billy was amazed that everywhere they went, Coach was greeted warmly. Mount Morris was a wonderful American town, and no one knew Chi was an ex-POW, except his close family. Don, Jr. had actually visited Honsfeld, Belgium on business. He described a conversation with an older gentleman who remembered seeing the bodies of American GIs in front of the barn. The young Don showed Billy pictures of the farmhouse and surrounding structures, and Bill said the structures were the same.

After their reunion, Billy and Chi spoke to each other every two weeks.

Eighteen months after they found each other, Billy got a call from Chi's wife, Angie. Angie told Billy that Coach had fallen down his cellar stairs. He had fractured his skull and died.

Billy was inconsolable. Why did God take him so soon after they were finally reunited?

"What if you had found Coach after he was already dead? God gave you to each other for 18 months," Billy's eldest son told him.

That was true about Goose. He had died in 1986 before Chi and Billy had found him and they were never reunited with him following the war.

MOUNT MORRIS

ATHLETIC
HALL OF FAME

Donald A. Chichester

- Teacher, Coach, Athletic Director at MMCS for his entire
  30-year career 1949-1979.
- One of Livingston County's and Section V's finest and most
  successful coaches.
- Coached a sport each season throughout his entire career.
- Coached 6 Section V Champion Baseball teams
- Coached 20 Livingston County Champion Baseball teams
- Won nearly 80% of all baseball games coached.
- Coached 3 Section V Champion Basketball teams
- Had over 300 victories in basketball in his career
- Section V Basketball Coach of the Year - 1975 and 1976
- Coached 1 Section V Champion Volleyball team

Inducted December 14, 2007

Three days after Chi's death, Billy and Rose flew up once again to Mount Morris to pay their respects at the wake and attend the funeral the next morning. At Chi's wake, the oldest son, Don Jr., asked Billy to deliver part of the Eulogy.

Billy was not a public speaker, but rather a simple man who was straight and to the point. He spoke from the heart to the packed assemblage. He spoke of the hard times he shared with Chi, the atrocities and the shared belief that the Almighty would see them through.

"I know Goose and Chi are together in God's paradise and will always be in my prayers as all the American POWs are. If I had another lifetime, I know I would never meet anyone like them. Their families should be very proud of them as I am to have known them. Gone but not forgotten, your buddy Billy will carry your memories for the rest of my life. God love you both."

He asked those present to whisper a prayer saying to Coach and to God, "Thank you for our Freedom."

23 9/11 SHATTERS THE LANG FAMILY

Many remember where they were on September 11, 2001. Shock, horror, sadness, and grief were just some of the emotions felt across the country and even the world. As fellow Americans were killed in the World Trade Center, the Pentagon, and that field in Shanksville, Pennsylvania, the nation was under attack and eyes were glued to television sets in disbelief.

But for Billy and Rose, their daughter, Rosanne, was missing on 9/11 and in the World Trade Center. For their eldest son, Billy Jr., and his wife, Paula, their son, Brendan (Billy and Rose's grandson),was also in the World Trade Center and missing on 9/11. Both Rosanne and Brendan were in separate towers of the World Trade Center.

They were never seen again. Both father and mother, and son and daughter-in-law shared the hardest loss of all on that fateful day: The loss of a child.

Billy and Rose's first-born daughter, Rosanne, was the seventh of their twelve children. Rosanne, 42, worked for Cantor Fitzgerald and was a successful institutional trader. So successful, in fact, that plans were in place for her to retire in two years. She was on the 102nd Floor of Tower One when the first plane hit the World Trade Center.

The second child of Billy Jr. and Paula, Brendan, 30, was the youngest Project Manager for an internal construction firm. He had completed five floors of executive offices in Tower Two. He called home as he witnessed the aftermath of the first plane hitting Tower One. He described the horrific scene in detail, including the people leaping from the upper floors to avoid being consumed by the flames.

Paula told Brendan, "Aunt Rosanne is in there." Brendan's last words to Paula was, "I have a plan, I love you." His father put on TV not two minutes after the call, just in time to watch the second aircraft kill his son.

Hundreds of calls to Rosanne's and Brendan's cell phones went unanswered. For the months following 9/11, voicemail introductions were still listened to, just to hear their voices, until both cell phone numbers were deleted by the carriers.

The hours of not hearing from Rosanne and Brendan, and not knowing if they had been killed was agonizing for the entire family, but more so for their parents.

Calls to area hospitals of whether they had anyone unidentified pulled from the wreckage from the World Trade Center were also futile.

The area hospitals were put on alert to accept massive injuries from the towers, but sadly there were not many people with injuries that needed to be in hospitals. Most people who were part of the horrific attacks were either the "walking wounded" or deceased.

Though the family held out for a miracle, as each day passed hope was dwindling.

Agonizing days of no communication took its toll. Posters were stapled across the city with pictures of Rosanne and Brendan, with "Missing, WTC" and phone numbers to call if they were seen or found.

The days after 9/11, with everyone keeping vigil at both parents' houses, resulted in many of the Lang siblings who could no longer sit and do nothing. One of Rosanne's brothers, Marty, a former fireman for the FDNY, announced he was heading to the site to look for Rosanne and Brendan. Three of his brothers also agreed to go. The day after 9/11, they were allowed entry to the site because of his FDNY credentials and dug through the rubble an entire day for their sister and nephew.

As they were at the site with professionals and other volunteers, word came to evacuate as the World Trade Center Building 5 was collapsing. They were forced to run from Ground Zero to escape injury.

Although they had hope, the realization of the inevitable came when they first approached Ground Zero.

The Lang family was forced to face the sad reality that Rosanne and Brendan were gone when New York officials announced the rescue mission had turned into a recovery mission.

Billy, Rose, Wullum and Paula resigned themselves to the fact they would never see, hug, kiss or speak to their beloved children.

While funerals could not be planned, as their remains were not recovered at that time, memorial services were planned separately for both members of the Lang family. The only hope the parents held onto was that they could give their children a proper burial and their remains would be somehow found.

Both Billy and Wullum decided to have separate memorials and funerals. Their children were each successful in their own spheres of influence. If grouped, there were just too many people to accommodate.

Both sets of parents had their cheeks swabbed for DNA analysis and sent to the New York Coroner's office to compare against remains that were being discovered at the site.

It took weeks, until October, before the Lang family could find some sort of closure in saying goodbye to Rosanne and Brendan. In their hometown of Middletown, N.J., churches were booked for weeks. Middletown lost 37 residents, the most people per capita outside of New York City.

Thousands turned out for each of their memorials and the emotional drain on bidding farewell to two family members took its toll.

Brendan and Rosanne were both declared "murdered" on their death certificates, and the Lang family mourned the death of two members of their immediate family. The weeks and months following 9/11 were filled with such grief and insurmountable pain.

Rosanne left behind a 17-year-old son, 11 siblings, her parents and countless nieces and nephews who loved her, not to mention hundreds of friends and co-workers whose lives she touched.

Brendan, who was married to his wife Sandy for only two years, left behind his parents, three siblings, cousins, friends and co-workers.

For those who he touched in life, Brendan left an indelible mark upon all their lives. Brendan's remains were recovered a few months after 9/11 and a funeral mass was held. A ceremony at the cemetery

was also held and his loved ones bid him a final farewell. His parents opted not to be notified if more remains were found.

Rosanne's remains were never found and a tombstone several hundred yards away from Brendan's sits atop an empty grave.

Every year, as the nation mourns and vows to never forget, a member of the Lang family goes to Ground Zero to read the names of Rosanne and Brendan.

Pictures of the towers continue to remind these parents of the greatest heartbreak that could be imagined. They are constantly bombarded by movies, newscasts, and commercials. The skyline of lower Manhattan now has the Freedom Tower majestically reaching skyward where the tragedy occurred. Beneath it lies the World Trade Center Museum and space for only the families to visit and grieve. Behind the wall of that space lie the remains of persons who could not be identified by DNA. Some believe their loved ones' remains have been lying in a dump on Staten Island where the deconstructed material was trucked.

Even the clocks show 9:11 twice every day and it seems that eyes are drawn to it, a cruel reminder of the victims of that fateful day.

While tragedy sometimes brings families closer together, 9/11 and circumstances surrounding it caused divisiveness in the Lang family, one of the closest of families.

For Billy and Rose, 9/11 tested their faith, as did the aftermath by the separation of some family members. The tragedy was beyond comprehension. But ironically, it was their faith once again that helped them get through the greatest loss a parent could experience.

24 BILLY'S ROSE BEGINS TO WILT

True love—what many hope they will attain in life but sometimes it could elude them—is what was Billy and Rose shared. Through countless hard times and numerous good times, their love for each other shined and deepened through the years.

Married for 67 years, the bond they shared was as soul mates. However, when Rose was diagnosed with Stage 4 lung cancer in 2014, Billy faced the hardest truth of all: He may lose the love of his life and a part of himself as well.

Rose was diagnosed and agreed to undergo chemotherapy treatments. They took their toll, but she continued to fight the disease that was ravaging her body. After she lost her hair and ordered a blonde wig, Billy winked at her and said, "Rose, you look great as a blonde. You should have gone blonde years ago."

Rose rolled her eyes at Billy.

While the chemotherapy did not eradicate her cancer, it did stop its spread for a period of time. But Rose, at age 83, continued to weaken. Her lashing out at Billy began to take its toll on him and he'd sometimes break down.

Doctors also tried targeted radiation therapy on Rose. After a year

and a half of both treatments, Rose was not certain she could go on.

Then a call on the morning of June 2015 made Rose consider finally giving up treatment.

Their son, Matthew, their eighth child, was found dead in his home at the young age of 53. Billy and Rose were inconsolable.

Another child of theirs died way too young and before his time.

Once again, their faith helped them deal with the tragic loss.

Rose, who had to attend the wake and funeral by wheelchair, looked so frail and her sadness at the loss of her son was unbearable. One only had to look at her eyes to see the pain and sorrow she was feeling.

After Matthew's funeral, Rose apparently was considering her own death and wrestling with a decision that would seal her own fate. She asked several of her children before making her decision if she should continue chemo and radiation treatment.

"I can't answer that for you, Mom," one of her children told her. "That's up to you."

"But the cancer isn't going away, and what quality of life do I have when I'm in bed all day?" she asked.

"If that's why you think, then you have to consider that when making your decision," her child said.

"Mom, I don't know what to say," another one of her children told Rose. "This is your decision and we'll stand by you no matter what you decide."

Rose and Billy talked about her condition and she ultimately decided to stop treatment in early August, weeks after Matthew's death.

Afterward, Rose continued a downward spiral and Billy saw his love, soul mate and a part of him start her descent on earth and her ascent into Heaven.

Billy and Rose started giving their children part of their inheritance. They were preparing for Rose's death.

In the final week and a half, Rose was confined to bed and hospice said it was only a matter of time. She was given morphine to keep her comfortable and her Billy, her children, and grandchildren all were visiting and staying with her during her final days.

When Rose finally took her last breath, most of her children and many grandchildren were present. Billy, who was downstairs at the time, was told Rose had finally passed.

Billy ran into their bedroom, broke down and cried, "My Rosie, my Rosie," and he held her one final time. Tears of sadness were on the faces of all those in the bedroom. A great woman had passed and the emptiness surrounded them.

They did, however, take some comfort knowing that Rose was no longer in pain and she was reunited with her daughter, son, grandchildren, and siblings.

The sheet was pulled over her face, and her son Richard took a rose from a nearby vase and placed it on her chest. Rose was taken to Heaven on August 23, 2015, only 10 weeks after her son's death.

When word spread throughout the family, many arrived to offer comfort and condolences. Their neighbors continued to bring endless food, more than could be consumed.

The mass was planned and a request was made for Father Carlos to say Rose's funeral mass. Carlos was the priest who Rose and Billy admired so much and who became close to them during his time at St. Mary's parish in Middletown, NJ. Carlos, who was transferred to a new parish several hours away, sought and was approved by both parishes to say her funeral mass.

Billy was elated upon hearing that the pastors approved of Carlos saying the mass.

Rose was given a beautiful send-off, and her daughter, Donna, sang her favorite song in church, "How Great Thou Art." Her grandchildren said the readings and lined up to each place a rose on her coffin.

After laying her to rest in the cemetery and a beautiful repast, Billy returned to an empty home. A pillow with a picture of her was what he held each night and even spoke to.

Billy was a lost soul after Rose's death. He would go to the funeral home with cases of soda for the directors whom he became friendly with. He also visited Rose's grave daily and made great friends with the cemetery workers.

For eleven months, Billy tried to continue without his beloved Rose, but he was in a depression and each day would say how much he missed her. But he told his children he would eat well and take care of himself because that was what she wanted.

Billy took care of business during those months following Rose's death. He purchased his coffin and he even picked out his suit and tie that he would be buried in. He also handed his children more of their inheritance.

He poured through photos that showed a lifetime of memories and also gave his children many of the pictures.

One Sunday morning after attending mass, he started having chest pains. He was brought to the emergency room and the doctors were monitoring him.

His children visited him and he was in good spirits. The doctors had planned to do a procedure for the following Tuesday morning to see if there were any blockages.

Billy died around 1 a.m. peacefully before they could do the procedure. Many of his children visited him that night as he lay in the hospital bed shortly after his passing. He looked finally at peace.

He died 11 months to the day that Rose died. It was August 23, which on the Catholic calendar was the Feast of St. Rose. That raised many eyebrows and some didn't believe his departure on the day was a coincidence.

Billy was given a hero's send off complete with Taps at the cemetery and police and firemen on nearly every street corner saluting his hearse.

People who did not even know Billy attended his wake. One man, who read that he had died, introduced himself. He said Billy had made a huge impression on his daughter when Billy recounted his World War II experience to her class and the man felt that he had to pay his respects.

The funeral directors were crying, as they became close to Billy after his wife's death. The cemetery workers all broke down as the man who became their friend over the previous eleven-month period would be sorely missed.

Many who bid farewell to Billy knew of him, knew him for a short period, or knew him for a lifetime. But one thing all agreed upon was that he was a man with distinction, a unique person whose pure heart and love was given freely.

The following song was sung at Billy's funeral mass by his son, Jamus, and it was one which resonated with all his children.

"The tears have all been shed now

We've said our last goodbyes

His soul's been blessed

He's laid to rest

And it's now I feel alone

He was more than just a father

A teacher my best friend

He can still be heard

In the tunes we shared

When we play them on our own

I never will forget him

For he made me what I am

Though he may be gone

Memories linger on

And I miss him, the old man."

--The Old Man, John McDermott

The love of God, family, and country were the cornerstones of his life, and it was one that could not be easily emulated.

The legacy that Rose and Bill left behind is immeasurable. Twelve children, 38 grandchildren, and 35 great-grandchildren (and counting), nieces, nephews, brothers and sisters, and countless friends and neighbors—all graced with their unconditional love.

ABOUT THE AUTHORS

William M. Lang III is a former IT professional, with four children and eight grandchildren who resides in Middletown, N.J. Mary Lou Lang is a freelance journalist who frequently contributes to the Washington Free Beacon. Her stories have also been published in The Daily Caller, LifeZette, and numerous other publications including financial magazines. She has two sons and resides in central New Jersey.

95999905R00066